Knotted

poems by

Lee Landau

Finishing Line Press
Georgetown, Kentucky

Knotted

Copyright © 2023 by Lee Landau
ISBN 979-8-88838-145-8 First Edition
All rights reserved under International and Pan-American Copyright Conventions. No part of this book may be reproduced in any manner whatsoever without written permission from the publisher, except in the case of brief quotations embodied in critical articles and reviews.

Publisher: Leah Huete de Maines
Editor: Christen Kincaid
Cover Art and Design: Maureen Alsop
Author Photo: Lisa Hlwya

Order online: www.finishinglinepress.com
also available on amazon.com

Author inquiries and mail orders:
Finishing Line Press
PO Box 1626
Georgetown, Kentucky 40324
USA

Table of Contents

From the Crayon Box 1
A Childhood Lisp 2
Never Family 3
Quacks 4
Echo from the Future 5
Eating Healthy 6
The Past, While Future Tense Screams Punishment 7
Grandmother's Poland 8
Foreign Vocabulary 9
Growing Rocks in Ruth's Garden 10
Man in the Mirror 11
Papa Purple 12
Midnight 13
Now Surgery 14
Marriage & the Beard 15
Shoes Bear a Familiar Design 16
Grandma Lena in the New World 17
Swarming Midwest 19
Stranger 20
Knotted 21
Tin Man and Scarecrow 22
Querido 23
Roberto & the Snow Globe 24
Sunlight Springs the Earth 25
Hopscotch 26
Living in the Past 27
Rafting the River 28

To Matthew, my son...you live in my heart

From the Crayon Box

Azure blue's morning
glories favorite. Just the color
for a sunlit sea,
coastal waters near Belize...
That same eye shadow
hue the morning's blush skyline
that requires tinted glasses.

Earthbound flowers—violets, irises,
where hydrangeas grow
swathed in blue, climbing
the lattice fence in this
side yard near
an awakened patch of
blueberries. Color palette's
never azured leaves
appear except

in the southern hemisphere.
This crayon box holds
more Avatar blue than the eye
can see, the childhood color
palette, primary
color's intolerable joy.

Childhood Lisp

Saturday morning
In ballet class,

        arms
        outstretched

    she
    slippers in,

taking her first
coltish steps,

now to study
the dance master

        for style
        and form,

    then stumbling,
    always leaping

to the wrong
conclusion.

Never Family

"Company first," you said,
keeping the freezer locked, daring anyone
to steal your hard work… always,
always for guests, *outside family*

like the rabbi's wife, glutton
for your butter cookies, her mouth,
an automatic blender. For Sabbath meals, we ate
chicken wings, never breast or drumstick
reserved for others.

I am here, meditating on the hunger
of a woman dying alone.
I swear I never wrote about Mother,
her days spent cleaning, always
ironing sheets and underwear,
hours cooking and baking for
the freezer, *never family.*

Mina, younger sister, sly bandito, persistent as
the bathroom's leaky faucet,
searched your purse, cabinets,
and kitchen drawers, found
the key to pans of lasagna, rugelach,

and those almond butter cookies.
Your grocery shopping after school,
how could you know?

Too late, yes, it was too late to stop
a daughter's feast.

Quacks

I still can't figure out your love of quacks,

the magic potions, weirded out, odd
treatments and equipment—those,

in essence, cure-alls for your 'sick' child.
Did you give up on orthodox, medical treatment,

the time it took me to relapse and recover from
pneumonia? Not your pain, discomfort, but mine.

How you tolerated the pain of electro-shock therapy
when I couldn't. Your daily enemas, back brace
for scoliosis, and arcane potions bled me out. What

about the magical X-ray machine used
to heal my scarred lungs... Remember
the knotted ilium, twin to your medical woes,
Father's asthma wheezing chorus, and
that last trip to Mt. Sinai Hospital:

radio blaring News Report, a flower of blood
poured from my mouth, lips blue. Underweight,
by 30 lbs., I lived in spite of you.

Echo from the Future

      Snowbound winter
threatens both roads. Fear
of what snow and ice
can do, where ice is the trajectory
speeding you up...
the past, a galloping horse, heedless
arrives at my door, races
ahead. But child,
you are my galloping horse
frozen to the past, how
to say farewell
over and over, as seasons change
against all this growth, this hoeing
choke weed back bent to the soil.

      Notice the peonies now
in a bottle, the guests, and you
adorned with white
roses selected for the death
of a child whose casket
remains closed—while swallows
crowd the gabled roof, their song
a fulsome noise
in tandem—your name
passing through these many
mouths.

Eating Healthy

She insisted on us
being vegan.

Cigarettes
and coffee, her first
two meals of the day, a diet
of thirty: three before breakfast
and lunch, three with coffee at
each meal, and outside
the house, we ate the mixed message
of lobster, beef, a cornucopia of banned
foods which meant we could break
any strict rules applied in the home.

Mother ate like a stevedore at dinner.
Sliding out of her night table,
a large can of mixed nuts and huge chocolate
bars were nibbled, ongoing through TV
until Johnny Carson, her time
to retire. Seeing
those treats turned me into
a whimpering pup: My allergies to nuts
and chocolate meant nothing to her, and
I sold out for that exquisite taste of
Belgian chocolate melting, the wheezing
asthma attacks following me to bed—
Sucking in the close air, sitting up,
shoulders hunched over, and lips,
that intense shade of blue...

I remember my mother for her eccentric,
eating habits. The Osterizer, faulty blender
pulped grape skins and pits, all vegetables
so thick our family had to chew them
just to swallow this drink.

The Past, While Future Tense Screams Punishment

She wants me off
the homebody reading floor, out
the door, more popular
at parties. That weekend, rare
invite to a sleepover—Elvis & Buddy Holly,
insane games and gossip.

Before leaving, I get my orders: clean
my bedroom, clear the closet floor
of everything. Yes. everything. My exception—
rubber-capped ice skates.

She knows my first move upon return,
to let my weekender go and the next,
the next moment she relishes—

Removing the rubber guards, she places the skates
blade side up, hides just inside
my comforter—vision of me
flopping on the bed, naked, the better
blades honed sharp
only three weeks earlier,
for rotating spins and jumps—

until stirring, my
growing breasts meet blades
and her blood-splattered jealousy.

Mother intends to teach me a lesson.

Grandmother's Poland

Poland,—
Such a tiny world
hemmed in by war,
pogroms and poverty
in a settlement
without a name
on the Polish border.
Russians seized
her oldest son, Joe,
fodder for the war machine.
Two sets of twins
died of starvation,
that season
wheat didn't grow.
Poles hunted down
the village women,
rape common like
those blue- eyed babies
rolling down an assembly line,
adopted into an Orthodox, Eastern
European culture.
The women prayed for sons
lest history repeat itself—
Daughters in black, widow weeds,
their futures already at risk
from a fiery mob.

Foreign Vocabulary
for the late Muriel Rukeyser

Gators are parked
around territory marked
as home front to her cottage.

¡Silence, *silencio!*
Dice el gato.

More than threats
to hoarse vocal cords,
words slur incomprehensible,
a foreign vocabulary—
Tongue flattened against the space
between her front teeth, whistling the wind
as a snake rattles its way
towards freedom, tall grass bending
sideways: s's, w's, z's
in her throat. Only a foreign
tongue remains audible
now. *Oui, oui,*
wags the dog to her snores,
a sweat soaked mattress
& dreams interspersed
with dullard sleep, locked
doors, windows still
perched open.

Tenga cuidad!
Dice el pero—take care.
Woof, woof
Danger in the yard.

Growing Rocks in Ruth's Garden
—for my mother-in-law

I will remember your fingers rooted in the earth,
a fiesta of wind and the summer rushing
at you—plucking chickweed, digging rooms
for hothouse pansies, transplanting wild daisies
for my rock garden.

You tame wildflowers with your winter song.
Swamp lilies, cattails danced off their stems again.
Another summer comes, comes on limpid breeze,
and I am here growing rocks, and what
flowers bloom hemorrhage overnight
like another you.

Man in the Mirror
—Father

His laughter spews outward in chortles
when hearing my jokes.

Slowly, the corners of his mouth tilt
upward, full lips closed. With eyes

half-open that mouth, stamped with
a smile, then blows mightily into the handkerchief.

A prominent Adam's apple genders him, shape
of eyebrows—see, even the wry eyes, above

and fleshy cheekbones, not quite jowls, stare
back at me, out from the mirror.

Papa Purple

Papa, the words come too hard,
you, playing Scrabble, cutting

the grass. Remember that
wet Sunday morning.

You chose to mow the lawn, when you
amputated your toe. We gathered

at the hospital certain of
your dying—allergic to the tetanus shot.

But you survived
Mama—and three daughters, your only
appendages, who weighed
you down.

When I was sick, we played Gin Rummy,
never talked. You worked, you worked
hard with nothing

left over for us, at
the mercy of an angry mother.

I remember
the leather strap you used on us,
our kaleidoscope scars,
because it was easier to follow
her orders than resist…

Midnight
> —by Ruby, the Asian elephant at the Phoenix Zoo-
> Four lithograph series. Lithograph #2.

Man eating tigers of the art world:

Think turquoise
Paradise Island waters, red
rocks of Sedona, yellows
of Thailand's people.

This spice road tastes of her
memory, this work often like 'found' art.

Loss of genius akin
to Einstein and Pollack, no
less a playwright than Shakespeare.
This school of the fifties
showcases her primary
colors plus pastel shadows, her canvas
large for its time.

Multicolor paint splashed across
attention from reviewers—Ruby's
backdrop—black to showcase acrylic
subject matter, and those distanced
from Ruby's success. Her strokes
reach out to this blackness
of a scooped, quarter moon night.

Now Surgery
>—*Mama, the thunder scares me.*

Words are displaced, their absence
part of a searchable frenzy to locate her face.

Plump lips, shortened nose, eyes
wide open, skin once wrinkled, now
smoothed out. Implants
contour her face, this my mother's
fourth surgery.

Plastic, plastique.
Like the wrecked family car
on blocks, photo prints, depression tied
to the bedposts in a thundering squall.
More knife knavery fighting off aging
unlike her mind,
concrete filler on bedrock.

Port of call, whoever can save her from aging.
Words and sputtered sounds form
in the fury from a jigsaw mind where
failures create a database of blank moments.

Elasticity gone like her youth: treated,
blooming lips ripen. Voluminous
hairdo stands on end, in spite
of no breeze or talc of sand.
Let's not discriminate:

Did you ever want to murder the now
crippled ex-husband, cry acid tears for
your dead daughter, try to cherish
the surviving son?

Marriage & the Beard

His mama told him to get hitched, to make her a grandma or she'd never speak to him again. He needed a "beard", also his large muscles in manly forearms to carry out his mother's wishes. He chose this bookworm. Virgin to play out his perfect performance, worthy of audience recognition. She had left a home too toxic, air too thin to breathe, chimera looks of parental dissatisfaction: Thinning bones, anxious smiles, old lady ways, and lank hair along with confused emotions. Freedom is so terrifying she chose a mama's boy, twenty-seven, educated, still living at home. How he showered her with concern, caring looks, bought her clothes to dress her up, stylish mannequin. Meanwhile, he loved, hated his darling backstory Mama, made her a grandma twice over. Fate or genes play out his next role's anonymous sex in men's highway restrooms. Wife and kids wait in the car, each stop, a betrayal.

Shoes Bear a Familiar Design
—What Changed in 1958?

Aging snows a storm
of implications—I feel alive, life made simple—
a skirt flared like a triangle and the shirt
forgotten, uninformed body parts stuck
to a shaky line with Minnie Mouse
shoes and Raggedy Ann hair.
The authentic me, the existential me—
Change fails to describe the relentless
storm, the open world earned, in spite of
paying the piper. My early twenties
absorbed gravity's rockslide.
I would draw myself as a stick figure, not
too different from early
childhood renderings: Thin lips
shape the mouth downward.

This relentless storm with
black and white streamers
rocking out the night
in Red Bank, New Jersey. Here
my older sister broke the color line:
*friends in school, but don't
socialize at parties. Don't date, don't
boyfriend Negros.* Between white
rock and roll, raucous joy,
Nat King Cole, B.B. King,
Motown mixed
those bodies up, some smoking
joints from the scent of it. Our lyrical
world of movement. Our twelve years
of schooling shared, friends now huddled
against her. By midnight,
"Coloreds" still traveled home, across
railroad tracks away from our white
neighborhood—driving
oh-so-slowly, avoiding
police detection.

Grandma Lena in the New World

I.
Davan Prayers

She practices
her American signature daily
tracing each loop and letter to cash
her 'widow' Social Security checks,
Her Yiddish words remain
an ongoing Rubik's Cube to

Three Anglo granddaughters,
and the weekly fat chicken bought
from the kosher butcher, mixed
chicken feet, embryo eggs,
all into the soup pot, always
on the stove.

This U.S. world was too big
for my grandmother: one
bath apartment with bed, barrel
chair, laundry scrubbed in the tub
then dried there on a rack and
a two-burner stove heating
her home.

Mother sends
penny postcards in Yiddish;
Lena returns in Yiddish postcards
with a nightmare of misspellings.

Only one
window connects her to this new
world where she gifts to the needy
not realizing her own
poverty, donating
a new pair of orthopedic shoes
meant for her swelling feet.

II.
Brooklyn Violent

On the Jewish stove
a huge pot of chicken soup
no matzoh balls, a fifteen-cent addition.

Chicken feet and unfertilized
eggs swimming to the top of boiling broth,
the skin saved, part of her breakfast,
to be fried with eggs for the next day.

Pots and pans live in the bathtub—share
space with laundry drying on a rack
Too proud to move, too sick to stay.

Saving coins in a glass ashtray, she
pays protection to the twelve-year old
down the hallway—half dollars & quarters
for her life? Elevators

smell like horse urine. Body odor
permeates her apartment door
like the twenty-five years
of stains on a sagging mattress.

Stuck in this volent,
changing neighborhood,
the ghetto, she can count on
the bedframe iron with bars
for a headboard.

Swarming Midwest

Major and minor notes late in the growing season.
Nebraska endures these years of dust and drought,

where nothing human stops their overhead passing,
this pestilence, the largest cloud of locust swarm over

a scoured land and hard worked fields by
 tired, aged generations. Minnesota's soil so sterile then,

their lives end with the same passing, ground
of bones. Who will mourn Nebraska, Kansas? Locusts,

as many as this loss—Discordant kind of music heard,
no hope, no crescendo notes fade from the dust

storms created. They will plant and pack the soil
with human bodies.

Stranger

You start up the ignition
just as the snow lays down its winter
storm to blind. So, the story: your eyes
missing the curved, unraveling highway
to light a joint.

Two kids in the back seat, ours,
fight to sit behind their dad.
Julie gets the window and already,
Osiris from the afterlife joins her.
Car careens out over the railing,
smashes into the concrete culvert below,
where a daughter, in too many, mangled
pieces leaves a son asleep deep in coma.

Then I meet a stranger to haunt me,
knocking on the front door, loud
enough to reach any god's ear, and

I call on who remains—
not the pot smoking dad, his
spine hips limbs, a puzzle
to piece together, but Him
the overseer, god of rebirth,
asking to return her
to me, if only for a while.

Knotted

Depression tied me to the bedpost.
   and my body shed icicles
      from a wild, strumming
         air conditioner…

Dire thoughts trembled
   in my scrambled mind
      product of shame.

While eyes soaked in regret
   could have filled a green lake.

Think of mounting wavelets
   storming the next lake
      like a procession of mourners
         bent on owning their sorrow.

Whole pieces of me dissolved
   screaming out lost egret soundings
      in the thundering squall
         of Julie, my daughter, dying.

Tin Man & Scarecrow

Off she went, in her ruby
shoes and tiara, wearing
a tulle skirt through
Kindergarten's opened doors.
The Wizard of Oz, for months
every night, she tethered me to
this book. But not even an hour

passed before the phone rang, her teacher
on the line...thoughts of injury burrowed
in. Mrs. King said my Julie insisted her name
was "Princess Dorothy," refusing
to answer to her given name.
I put down the teacher's concerns,
cheered my child's imagination:

Four years old, her dancing
steps focused on new friends.
She begged me for a good witch,
Glinda wand, ruby-red slippers, even
renamed our dog, Toto. After all,
dancing munchkins might populate
the path to our front door,

her chrysalis mind, reborn.

Querido
    —remembering Roberto

We test our hunger for one another.

At Murphy's Bar
body heat and feral cat
romping in the snow,
we dance Bolero, hips
glued to Latino music
ready to claw one another
out of control, bar

closed, we play, pleasure
in the ripples with each touch,
drawing on blood and passion—
You enter my dark room, pressing
your face to every part
of me, inhaling the heathen
moment, who wrestles

with need and a new language.

Roberto & the Snow Globe
—after Margaret Atwood

This world you took
away with you

so small, a snow globe fit
in your callused hand.

Snow perplexing
a visible-blue sky,

branches shaking
from the weight of it.

Here trees crawl like spiders
to catch the wind.

Not unlike this snow globe,
where you, in white relief, survive.

Only the ground hints of
substance, more like your

outcropping of rock, this
hardening ghost echo.

Snow shapes you with
no vocabulary left to dance

around danger where once
my tongue left flakes. Soon,

only snow will be visible,
our love shaken apart.

Sunlight Springs the Earth

So much fortitude
in the greening of Spring, this bevy
of flowers growing in bogs,
Sumac, Anemone and Amarillo.
Alongside daffodils
a field of crocus blooms.
What else marks Springtime's early goslings,
the calving near our barn
doorway? Daisies begin
to posture like a group of overrun,
wild blossoms bursting open.

The Sun's own vivid yolk sunny side up,
yet weak as the paleness of gouda cheese.
Then a random event
intermixed with gray skies and rain,
warmer rain to quench garden
plantings, and scores of
unruly flowers in that bog
alongside poison ivy, the color faded,
purple irises.   So much promise—
wild growth chokes
human plantings, overruns these
fields of dandelions
until June sun
crushes a rash of
uninvited daisies and asters.

The hills, all of it
new greening again for
another season.

Hopscotch

I'll go first.
Pretend, pretend
until childhood's end,
swim in the iridescent ocean
near shore, my hands
on the bottom, feet kicking.

Hopscotch is a word.
Let's have fun.
You swim, you win!
Let's play Checkers.
I win, I win your kings.
or monopoly, you win
my money, bankruptcy & tears.

Sixteen, eighteen, twenty-one,
try again the sack race.
Fall down laughing,
then get up to start
the next phase.

When does this world convert
children to men?
Adult, adult—
Pretend, pretend!

Living in the Past

The porch wide slat pine floor
creates its own music
to rock away the blues—
My younger sister hears notes
harsh with the rasp
of bass and trumpet, interspersed
with the honey of a tenor sax,
as memories sync to the rhythm
of her rocking chair—paint peeling,
ladder back with cane seat, holding
only its one arm, the other broken off
too many years ago

like attacks on her flesh, fear
of pain. Eyes closed, she rakes through
the past collecting jazz notes
for the moment.

A wealth of jazz history
exhaustion playing counterpoint
to a ticking clock...
Pain panics her mind.

No husband or children,
my younger sister tries to
retrieve something
from her exhaustion
numb to the future, even I
cannot own.

Rafting the River

> *"Maybe more poems should drown instead of being broadcast at poetry readings. Picture their endings, predictable fatalities". —Maxine Kumin*

My poem's ending
is caught hanging from
the abandoned fishing line
until Dan's paddle pushes hard
to release it, watch
wavelets churn into the current
then disappear.

Dan, skint with a dollar,
packed in brine, his joy rationed,
could be rafting the Hudson River upstate.

White water smashes rocks
midstream, careens
into these cross currents and whirlpools.

Beginnings are simple, second marriage
hard, coupling conflict and gravitas,
how our needs differ.

With each sport he conquered,
I risked my life, for this poem, at every
broken plank landing
coming into view.

NOTES

Perro and gato: dog and cat in Spanish

Rugelah: a sweet, crusty pastry stuffed with prune or apricot preserve

ECT: Electro Shock therapy to the brain to brighten one's perspective on living

Osiris: God of the After Life and rebirth

Daven: The ritual act of bowing in praise of GOD while praying

ACKNOWLEDGMENTS

A number of poems originally appeared in a different form:

Open Minds Quarterly. Reprint. Her Sadness Unmasked (The Past, While Future Tense Screams Punishment)
Bluestockings Magazine at Brown University. Eating Healthy
Burningword Literary Journal. Feral Cat (Querido)
Broad Street Magazine. Me Not You, Mother (Quacks)
Rockhurst Review. Mind Body Connection (Knotted)
Else Where Lit. Karen's Jazz Notes (Living in the Past)
Breath and Shadow. The Past a Galloping Horse (Echo from the Future)
Ice Box Journal. A Childhood Lisp
Broad River Review. Roberto and the Snow Globe
Cease Cows. Never Family

Contest Awards:
—Honorable Mention. *New Millennium Writings*. "Aunt Betty's Legacy"
—LOMP. *Writ in Water* Poetry Contest. Certificate of Merit. "Rafting the River."
—Rash Award Finalist. *Broad River Review*. "Roberto and the Snow Globe."
—Finalist at *Poetica Magazine*, the Anna Rosenberg Prize: "Sitting Shiva."

Lee Landau has been writing poetry since the age of twelve. She is now 78 years old. Her first chapbook, *Knotted*, will be published early in 2023. She developed and manages a growing network of 1500 poets on LinkedIn.com. Her poetry has been published in *Poetica, New Millennium Writings, bluestockings* at Brown University, *Broad River Review* and the *Poetic Bond Anthology* to name a few. She identifies as a feminist. Known influences through her participation in poetry workshops: Billy Collins, Tom Lux, Maxine Kumin, Sharon Olds. Her own work continues to evolve. She is currently completing her second chapbook, where she resides in Florida on the Gulf coast.

www.ingramcontent.com/pod-product-compliance
Lightning Source LLC
Chambersburg PA
CBHW022124090426
42743CB00008B/995